50 Gems for the Journey
Lessons for Everyday Wins

By Dominique Giggz

Self-Published
ISBN: 979-8-218-59607-1
Printed in the United States of America

First Edition: January 2025

Disclaimer:
This book is a work of nonfiction. The author has made every effort to ensure accuracy, but the publisher assumes no responsibility for errors or omissions. All opinions expressed are solely those of the author.

Dedication

"To my beloved mother, whose strength and resilience taught me the essence of true strength and womanhood—your memory inspires me daily. To my father, my hero, whose unwavering love remains a guiding light in my life—thank you for being my constant source of strength and wisdom."

About the Author

Dominique Giggz's story is as unique and inspiring as the wisdom in this book. Born in Schwäbisch Gmünd, Germany, but raised in St. Louis, MO, Dominique's life has been a rich tapestry of varied experiences, profound lessons, and unyielding resilience. Dominique learned early the value of strength, adaptability, and cherishing life's fleeting moments. The nickname "Giggz" came from Dominique's signature laugh, a sound that has always surfaced whether she is happy, mad, or sad. It's a name that was given to her and stuck like a badge of honor. It symbolizes an enduring presence that finds light even in the darkest corners of life. Dominique's faith in God has underpinned her fortitude, regardless of how tough life has been. Through trials, her faith has been her North Star that guides her to know that every storm comes with a lesson and that every setback serves a divine purpose. Dominique's journey has not been easy. Through all of life's challenges and setbacks, the most significant lesson learned from the journey has been wisdom. Artistic expression from a young age with an interest in creating art, poetry, writing, and music has always been a component of her existence that has served as the backdrop of a foundation that evolved into a greater purpose: Sharing her experiences and wisdom that may help others get through life. 2011 Dominique took a leap of faith, leaving St. Louis to travel across the U.S. for work. These travels have developed into a cauldron for growth, forging an affinity for self-discipline and positivity's unique impact on our experiences. From the serene beauty of Hawaii to the bustling vibrancy of California and nearly every state in between, Dominique embraced new cultures, perspectives, and the universal truth: no matter where you go, your mindset is the most powerful tool you have.

Dominique's vision for '50 Gems for the Journey' was clear from the start: to create a book anyone could relate to, from someone living paycheck to paycheck—or no paycheck at all—to someone who seems to have it all but struggles to find happiness. This book is for anyone trying to become the best version of themselves. Through countless experiences—some good and some difficult—Dominique learned the one thing she has benefited from is that success is not a measure of how much money you have; it's measured by how many times you get up, stay positive, have the faith, and dare to continue putting one foot in front of the other. This book is the realization of those lessons, a guide for anyone who needs affirmation to continue moving ahead. Dominique would like '50 Gems for the Journey' to inspire fire in every reader, reminding them that greatness is possible and achievable even from rock bottom. If you are determined to grow, it will guide you to your highest peak. Let this book act as your companion, cheering you on through every step toward a life that's not merely a struggle to survive but a victory.

Introduction

Welcome to 50 Gems for the Journey. This book is designed to inspire, uplift, and guide you toward everyday wins. Each gem offers actionable lessons, drawn from my personal experiences, to help you overcome challenges and find joy in the process. Whether you're looking to rebuild from setbacks or reach new heights, these gems are here to empower you every step of the way.

Gem 1

Your Mental Playlist

Your thoughts are like playlists—what you keep repeating in your mind sets the vibe for your life. If you're steadily playing doubt and negativity, don't be shocked when your life feels like a depressing soundtrack. Every lyric in your head—every loop of inner dialogue—sets the tone for how you move through the day. Decide what you put into your head. Imagine songs that you wake up to that lift you instead of pulling you down. What if, instead of replaying your setbacks or where you went wrong, you focused on affirmations, accomplishments, and the goals you are working for? Put confidence, discipline, and love on your mental playlist and see how your perspective shifts.

Here's something worth considering: We don't always realize where the tracks on our mental playlist come from. Sometimes, they're put there by someone else, a parent, a boss, or even a toxic relationship. Their negativity could be played on repeat without you even realizing it. The great thing is that you can hit "delete." Replace those tracks with ones that remind you of your strengths, goals, and worth.

And remember, the best playlists don't stay the same forever. Keep adding new tracks that reflect who you're becoming. As you grow, so should the energy you carry. That old track of "I can't" or "I'll never" doesn't belong in the person you're becoming. You're the DJ, the producer, and the audience of your life. Curate wisely.

Takeaway Quote: "What you repeat in your mind sets the vibe for your life. Stop playing doubt and negativity—switch to confidence, discipline, and love, and watch your vibe change."

Gem 2

Choose Peace Over Pettiness

Everyday life will throw mess your way—folks cutting you off, people talking slick, bills piling up. It's easy to let it all pile onto your spirit until you feel heavy, angry, and ready to snap. But here's the secret: you've got the power to choose peace over pettiness.

Think of peace like a savings account. Every time you choose not to engage in drama, you're making a deposit. When you protect your energy, you build wealth in the calm currency. Okay, snapping back feels good, but is that the payoff? What do you gain from someone else's stupidity? Here's the thing: it becomes very clear to others when you choose peace as your norm. It's like walking into bedlam in an unfortunate garment — something silky. It takes people by surprise, and then the tide turns in your favor.

Protect your energy like it's your last $20 on a Friday night—not because peace is weak, but because it's power.

The real flex isn't who can throw shade better. Who can walk away unbothered, with their spirit untouched and their joy intact? Trust me—peace pays better than pettiness ever could.

Takeaway Quote: "Life will throw mess your way, but don't let it sit in your spirit. Avoid pettiness and treat your energy like the last $20 on a Friday night."

Gem 3

Mastering the Art of Unbothered

In life, there may be people who will test you. Whether it's someone cutting you off in traffic, throwing shade at work, or trying to provoke you elsewhere, the goal is to knock you off your square. But here's the power move—don't let them. Being unbothered isn't just a mindset; it's a flex that no one can take from you.

Imagine a scenario: chaos is breaking loose around you. Someone's trying to get under your skin, daring you to hit back, but rather than lashing out, you stay quiet. You don't talk back, you don't retaliate. You are so incredible that their ruckus is just background music. That's the beauty of not being bothered; you rob them of their power and magnify your power.

Here's the twist: to be unbothered is not to be indifferent or passive. It means you love your peace so much that you're not letting anybody break it. But it's just a matter of realizing that every battle doesn't need to be fought, and every comment doesn't need a response. Your energy is sacred, and how you share it is your choice.

Remaining unbothered is a craft, a tactic, and, frankly, a superpower. It keeps you focused on what is truly important: your goals, your growth, your greatness. Let those who doubt, doubt, those who hate, hate, and chaos swirl. You've been busy winning in the meantime.

Takeaway Quote: "Not caring is the greatest flex. Let people test you, talk slick, throw shade — it's nothing but background noise to your greatness."

Gem 4

Controlling Emotions

Don't let temporary feelings make you ruin permanent blessings. Life moves fast, and emotions hit hard, but they don't have to control you. Think of emotions like a thunderstorm in the middle of St. Louis weather—wild, unpredictable, but always temporary.

Here's the twist: emotions aren't the enemy. They're messengers. Anger might be telling you about boundaries that need setting. Sadness might be pointing out areas that need healing. Sit with them instead of running from them or letting them drive your actions. Listen, learn, and let them pass.

Impulse can feel powerful, but wisdom is more potent. The next time you feel overwhelmed, breathe. Take a moment. Remember that you're more significant than the storm. And remember, the sun always comes back out; it's just a matter of time.

Takeaway Quote: "Don't let temporary feelings wreck permanent blessings. Breathe, slow down, and remind yourself: emotions don't control you—you control them."

Gem 5

Hustle in Silence

The loudest moves get the most hate. Ever notice how people who brag about their next big thing tend to face the most obstacles? That's because when you put your plans out too soon, you invite unwanted energy—jealousy, doubt, and sabotage.

Here's the twist: hustling in silence is not merely avoiding showing your moves — it's about silently building your confidence. The way to mega-success is not always an in-your-face presence; sometimes, just showing up and letting your results do the talking resonates infinitely more. It's like arriving to the playoffs as an underdog and leaving as a champion.

You don't need an audience, live or otherwise, for your journey. Focus on your grind, let people sleep on you, and then show up so undeniably that they can't look away.

Takeaway Quote: "The loudest moves get the most hate. Hustle in silence, let them sleep on you, and then show up like the playoffs are unmissable."

Gem 6

Trust the Reroute

Every setback isn't a sign to quit; sometimes, it's God rerouting you to better streets. When one door closes, don't cry at the threshold—turn around because there's an entire block of opportunity waiting.

Life is like driving through a city with road construction everywhere. You've got your destination in mind, but suddenly, the GPS says, "Rerouting." Frustrating, right? But here's the thing: sometimes, the detour takes you up a nice or more beautiful road. Consider a time when something didn't work out, a job that didn't change hands, a relationship that ended, a plan that unraveled. It probably felt like failure at that point. Yet, in hindsight, didn't things ultimately work out for the better? Sometimes there's beauty in a reroute. You may not always see the blessings to come, but they are there.

So, don't slam on the brakes when life detours you. Trust the process, adjust your path, and keep moving forward. The road ahead might have the view you've been praying for.

Takeaway Quote: "Setbacks aren't signs to quit—they're God's way of rerouting you to better streets. Don't cry at the closed door; a whole block of blessings is waiting."

Gem 7

Building Lasting Relationships

In a relationship, it's not you versus them; it's the two of you versus the world. Trust, two-way communication, and mutual respect are the foundations of any long-lasting relationship; authentic relationships are built on these. It's not about keeping score or scoring points; it's about building something solid, and then the outside forces can't shake it.

It's like a house: A good foundation is essential; even the best-built houses require maintenance. Often, the minor cracks, the unseen problem, ruin a deal. Building a relationship takes regular check-ins and purposeful work to maintain.

In today's world, relationships often feel like they're built for show—measured by likes or appearances. But real connections aren't about the surface, whether with your partner or friends. They're about being each other's safe space, building together, and keeping outside noise exactly where it belongs—outside.

Takeaway Quote: "Relationships aren't built for the 'Gram— they're built for real life. Whether love or friendship, build each other up, stack blessings together, and keep the outside noise where it belongs—outside."

Gem 8

Dreams Require Action

Wishing without doing is like putting rims on a car without a motor. It looks nice but it's not going anywhere. Until you take action, you are just dreaming and doing nothing about it. The catch is that dreaming big is only part of the solution. The other half? The grind.

Consider your dream to be a vintage car parked in your garage. It's glossy, abundant with potential, and eager to hit the road. It's only a beautiful idea until you hit the gas, turn the key, fill the tank, and steer the next mile. Each small step you take gets you closer to your dreams. So, turn the ignition. Stay low-key, focus on the mission, and grind until your dreams are your home.

Takeaway Quote: "Dreams without work are like rims on a car with no engine—they look good, but they aren't going anywhere. Put in the work and drive toward your goals."

Gem 9

Redefining wealth

Real wealth isn't just money; it's in peace, time, and who you share it with. Stack your coins, but don't forget to stack your joy and memories.

Here's the twist: society will have you chasing a dollar, thinking it's the only measure of success. But what's the point of having a fat bank account if your soul feels bankrupt? Real wealth is being able to laugh with your loved ones, sleep peacefully at night, and wake up excited for the day ahead.

Yes, get your bag. Secure your financial future. But don't let the grind take away the moments that matter. True wealth lies in the equilibrium between aspiration and gratitude. Pursue the life that makes you feel alive, not just the paycheck.

Takeaway Quote: "Real wealth is not just money; it's peace, time, and the people you share it with. Stack your coins, but don't forget to stack your joy."

Gem 10

Don't Sweat the Small Stuff

The little things aren't so little when you let them steal your happiness. Somebody taking your parking spot, a slick comment on social media, or someone cutting in line—none of it is worth losing your peace.

Here's the twist: those little annoyances are like mosquitoes. They're small, but if you focus on them too much, they'll drive you crazy. The secret is learning to brush them off before they take over your day.

Whenever you let go of the petty stuff, you're reclaiming your joy. And here's the truth: happiness is too expensive to let small things steal it. Keep your energy on what matters, and let the rest go. Life is too short for drama.

Takeaway Quote: "Small stuff isn't worth your peace. Let that parking spot go, ignore the Facebook drama, ignore what he or she hearted on Instagram, and keep your happiness intact—it's too expensive to lose."

Gem 11

Haters Only Throw Shade Because You're Shining

Haters only throw shade because they can't handle your light. If they're talking about you, congratulations—you're officially doing something worth noticing. Think about it: nobody wastes their breath on someone irrelevant. When you shine, it makes insecure people uncomfortable, but that's their problem, not yours.

Here's the twist: haters are like unintentional hype teams or free billboards. They give you free exposure and marketing whenever they mention your name. It's like they're handing out flyers to your success. Instead of getting caught up in their negativity, treat it like noise in the background—annoying, but it doesn't stop the show. The brighter your light, the harder they'll try to throw shade, but here's the secret—they can't dim what's destined to shine.

So let them talk, roll their eyes, or throw their little jabs. None of that noise can block what's meant for you. Success speaks louder than opinions; they'll talk for you when your blessings appear.

Takeaway Quote: "Let them talk—it's free advertising. Haters are just confused fans who don't know how to cheer properly. Keep shining; they can't block what's meant for you."

Gem 12

Success Isn't for the Lazy

Success is like trying to catch the bus—you hear them pulling off, and you'll miss it if you're not running. Nobody's holding the door open, waiting for you to catch up. Lazy doesn't cut it, and excuses are just distractions in disguise.

Here's the twist: Effort isn't optional. Success doesn't care about how tired you are, how unfair life feels, or how much you want it to be easier. It only responds to action. Imagine seeing the opportunity before you and letting it slip away because you weren't willing to hustle. That's not the life you want.

Get up. Move. Hustle like your future depends on it—because it does. You don't want to be like, 'What if I'd done more?'

Takeaway Quote: "Success isn't for the lazy. Hustle as if the bus is not waiting on you."

Gem 13

Your Mindset is Your GPS

Your mindset is the navigation system for your life. If you're stuck thinking small, you'll end up on the same block, circling the same streets, wondering why nothing's changing. But when you think big, you open the highways of opportunity and success.

And here's the plot twist: Recalibrating is not failing—it's growing. When you get lost, just as your GPS re-adjusts the planned route provided by a better path, your mindset will lead you in the right direction. Perhaps you've been stuck in traffic, repeating the same patterns, but it's time to detour. Cultivate higher aspirations, aim higher, and do not agree to expedients that amount to dead ends.

The destination awaits, but you're completing the course. Don't play small; think about what you deserve — aim for what you know you can get.

Takeaway Quote: "Your mindset is your GPS. Big dreaming and recalibrating plans on the go will pave your way to success."

Gem 14

Stop Comparing Your Grind

Seeing someone else's highlight reel will make you feel poor, unsuccessful, and unworthy. But here's the thing: You don't know their real story. You're seeing the highlights, the wins, not the late nights, sacrifices, or tears that got you there."

Comparison is a thief. And it steals your joy, focus, and momentum. You rob your energy with every glance at someone else's progress. Stay true to yourself, keep hustling, and always keep in mind that your journey is one of a kind. You are the hero of your own story, not an incidental extra in someone else's.

Keep pushing forward. Your highlight reel will eventually inspire you to believe in your future, with every move and choice shaping the path ahead.

Takeaway Quote: "Stop comparing your grind to somebody else's highlight reel. Focus on your story; you're the main character, not a background extra."

Gem 15

Find a Crew That Claps

Your circle should be your loudest cheerleaders. You're sitting at the wrong table if your wins are met with silence or side-eyes. Real friends celebrate your success like their own, hyping you up and pushing you to go even further.

Here's the twist: the wrong circle can drain you. People who secretly compete with you or get jealous when you shine will only hold you back. Watch who stays quiet when you win—that silence is louder than any applause. Your people should inspire you, push you, and clap for you like they're in the front row of a concert.

Find a crew that's rooting for you, not against you. Life is better when surrounded by people who celebrate your growth, share your wins, and support your dreams.

Takeaway Quote: "If your circle isn't clapping for your wins, it's time to find a new crew. Real ones celebrate like they scored, too."

Gem 16

Real Strength is Quiet

True strength isn't about showing off for the audience; it's about weathering the storms that seek to take you down. It's sobbing alone but walking into a room with your head high and emotions intact. Strength is not loud; it is steady, quiet, and unshakeable.

Here's the catch: The strongest people are not the ones who never fall; they're the ones who always get back up. Their scars are stories of survival, and their smiles are evidence that the storm was lost. It is not easy, but true strength drives elegance through this world, even when life decides to throw punches.

Keep smiling. Keep pushing. You don't have to show the world your struggles; they will witness your strength through your actions.

Takeaway Quote: "The strongest people aren't the ones flexing; they're the ones who smile after surviving the storm."

Gem 17

Forgiveness is Freedom

Holding onto old resentments is like swimming with shackles; you only hold yourself back. Forgiveness is not about letting the other guy off the hook but liberating you.

Here's the tricky part: forgiving doesn't mean forgetting or condoning bad behavior. It means not allowing that pain to govern your present or future. The energy it takes to hold onto anger is the energy you could use to build your dreams, love your life, and create new memories.

Let it go—not for them, but for you. When you release the grudge, you make space for peace.

Takeaway Quote: "Forgive for yourself, not for them. Letting go isn't weakness; it's freedom."

Gem 18

Tunnel Vision Wins

There are distractions everywhere, and they will kill your progress if you don't beat them to it. Social media, drama, and clout-chasing are potholes — they feel small, but too many will bump you out of alignment.

Here's the catch: staying focused doesn't mean tuning out the world; it means tuning into what matters. Your goals deserve your focus; everyone else is just noise to tune out.

Stay focused, stay locked in, and let your results speak. Distraction doesn't spotlight your focus; it muffles it.

Takeaway Quote: "Be so focused on your goals that distractions are unappealing. Tunnel vision leads to wins, not likes."

Gem 19

Lessons in the L's

Win or lose, you ultimately learn something from everyone around you. Every one of those struggles is a steppingstone, not a setback. Ask what you can understand instead of complaining about what didn't work.

Here's the twist: the most successful people in the world did not arrive at success without failure. They absorbed the lessons from every failure, adapted, and pressed on. Once you learn the lesson, you reward yourself by leveling up from it.

Your defeats are not the be-all and end-all; they are the blueprint for your subsequent victory. Take the lesson, and let it strengthen you.

Takeaway Quote: "Every bad day hides a lesson. Stop complaining, start learning, and turn L's into levels."

Gem 20

Motivation Meets You Halfway

Waiting for motivation to show up is like waiting for rain in a drought—it's not coming. Motivation doesn't knock on your door; it meets you halfway. You must take the first step, even when you don't like it.

Here's the twist: action creates momentum, and momentum creates motivation. Start small—one step, one task, one goal. The more you move, the easier it gets. Waiting is a trap; doing is the solution.

You must get up and get going; motivation will follow you. You'll be amazed at what you can achieve when you stop waiting and start working.

Takeaway Quote: "Motivation is not Amazon Prime — it will not be delivered. Just start moving, and it will meet you halfway."

Gem 21

Be Your Hero

Life doesn't owe you anything, but you owe yourself everything. Stop hoping that someone will come and rescue you. All you need is your strength, resilience, and determination. You are the superhero you have been waiting for.

Here's the twist: heroes are not born in the spotlight but forged in struggle, lonely nights, and silence. You don't need a cape and a crowd cheering you on. You only need the strength to step up for yourself when no one else can.

The ability to transform your life resides within you. You start to soar when you stop waiting for a rescue and start taking action.

Takeaway Quote: "Life doesn't owe you anything, but you owe yourself everything. Stop waiting for a rescue—be your hero."

Gem 22

Remember Why You Started

When the struggle is too real and throwing in the towel seems easier, take a moment to remember why you started. That dream, that goal is still there, right before you on the other side of the difficult days.

But here's the twist: Think of your career journey as a road trip. Quitting is halfway. You go through all this time to make it halfway; why waste it? And with every step you take, you get one step closer to the finish line, and victory makes every obstacle worthwhile.

When the road looks steep (and I mean steep), keep walking. You didn't start this race ahead of the finish.

Takeaway Quote: "Somedays are hard, and you want to quit. The struggle is real, but so it is the reward."

Gem 23

Growth isn't Comfortable

Growth doesn't come with comfort—it comes with challenges. It's like wearing shoes a size too small; it feels tight, pinches, and awkward, but eventually, you outgrow what no longer fits.

Here's the twist: you can't make room for blessings if you still hold onto old habits, toxic people, and outdated mindsets. Growth demands that you let go of the things that keep you small, even when they hurt.

It's challenging, but the discomfort is short-lived. And by the time the blessings you've been praying for come your way, the new version of you preparing for the place of abundance on the other side of all that growing pain will make everything worth it.

Takeaway Quote: "Growth isn't comfortable, but you have to. Release what no longer serves you to create space for your blessings to come."

Gem 24

Progress is Still Progress

Progress is Still Progress. Not being where you want to be doesn't equal failing. Even slow progress is still progress. Impatience should not rob you of the pride of the journey you have taken thus far. But here's the wrinkle: Life is not a sprint; it's a marathon. You run; some days, you walk, but every little thing counts. Celebrate your small wins as they lead to your big wins.

And keep working for it because we think it will never come. The only people who lose are those who have never played the game.

Takeaway Quote: "Progress is still progress, no matter how slow. Just keep moving; you're lapping everyone who is still upright."

Gem 25

Treat Your Dreams Like Rent

Your dreams are non-negotiable, just like your rent. If you want them to stay alive, you've got to show up every day and do the work. Excuses don't pay the bills and won't build your dreams, either.

Here's the twist: treat your dreams like the landlord is knocking. Work like eviction is on the line because, in a way, it is. The world won't wait for you to get it together—your hustle determines whether you succeed.

Dreams only thrive when you feed them with consistent effort. Keep showing up, and watch how far you can go.

Takeaway Quote: "Treat your dreams like rent—non-negotiable. Work like evictions on the line, and success will be yours."

Gem 26

Prove Yourself Right

When people doubt you, please don't waste your energy trying to prove them wrong. Instead, focus on establishing yourself right. Your success will silence the doubters far better than any argument ever could.

Here's the twist: the best revenge isn't a clapback—it's a clap for yourself. Doubters love to distract, but you're building something they can't take away every time you redirect that energy into your grind.

Let your results speak louder than their words. They'll have nothing to say when you're standing on your success.

Takeaway Quote: "When folks doubt you, don't waste time proving them wrong. Prove yourself right, and your success will handle the rest."

Gem 27

Protect Your Table

Not everyone who sits at your table is there to eat with you. A few come to remove your plate. Because there is no need to hustle, be careful who you let in your circle and defend what you sacrificed time to create.

Here is the twist: loyalty is not just in your words but your actions. See who applauds your achievements, who stays at your side when the going gets tough, and who brings something to the banquet. Life is too short to give your time to people who will suck your energy.

Surround yourself with people who bring value to your table, not just appetite.

Takeaway Quote: "Be mindful of who you let sit at your table. Real ones bring something to the feast; the rest want to take your plate."

Gem 28

Start Where You Are

Success is a climb, not an elevator ride. Nobody wakes up on top—you've got to start where you are, use what you have, and take it step by step.

Here's the twist: every step matters, even the small ones. The climb might be slow, but every bit of progress gets you closer to the top. Don't get discouraged by how far you have to go— be proud of how far you've already come.

The only failure is quitting. Keep on going, and you will reach heights you never thought existed.

Takeaway Quote: "Nobody wakes up on top. Success is a climb — you begin at the base and keep climbing up."

Gem 29

Let Them Laugh

They're the same people laughing at your hustle now, as they will one day envy your grind. Let them laugh and use that as fuel for your fire. Keep your head down, keep your face out of a brag book, and never feel sorry for shining.

The truth is that people laugh at what they don't comprehend, and that's not your dilemma. Your grind is not to have them approve of your goals. Just continue to show up with all your shiny, new, successful self and let it hopefully speak for itself.

One day, they will quit laughing and inquire how it happened. By then, you will be too busy winning to pay attention.

Takeaway Quote: "The same person laughing at your grind now will envy your success later. Keep shining — your light doesn't need permission."

Gem 30

The Resilient Mindset

Life is not for the faint of heart, no matter your backdrop. The motto for anyone trying to overcome hard work, staying firm, and not letting your struggles defeat you. This isn't merely about weathering something; it's about flourishing.

The plot twist: the struggle isn't the ending; it's the resilience plan. Success will find you if you stay committed, true to yourself, and focused on your path.

This way of thinking is not location-specific; it's global. No matter where you're from or what you face, the formula is the same: work with purpose, stay grounded, and allow the rest to align.

Takeaway Quote: "The resilient mindset is simple: work hard, stay solid, and never let the struggle defeat the spirit. The rest will fall into place."

Gem 31

Trust the Process

When God places something in your heart, it's not by accident! The vineyard may not resemble your dream tree house, but the grapes are always worth it. Believe that His timing is perfect, even when it seems slow.

Here's the twist: God's process is much like barbecue — it's slow, intentional, and always worth the wait. Don't rush it: every hang-up, every wander off the path, all a recipe for something great.

Stay faithful and keep pushing. The best is yet to come.

Takeaway Quote: "When God places something in your heart, believe in the process. The journey may not look how you thought it would, but the destination is always worth it."

Gem 32

Your Environment Shapes Your Growth

Your environment can shape who you are and who you become. Think of yourself as a plant; no matter how strong your roots are, you can't thrive in bad soil. If the people around you constantly bring negativity, drama, or doubt, it's no wonder you feel stuck. You need to be in a space that feeds your growth, not starve it.

Here's the twist: the people around you influence you in ways you might not notice. If dreamers, doers, and believers surround you, their energy will fuel your fire. But if your circle is full of doubters, complainers, and energy vampires, they'll drain your potential before it can bloom.

Altering your surroundings doesn't require disconnecting from everyone you know, but it does mean being deliberate about who you spend time with. Surround yourself with people who motivate you to be better, who celebrate your victories, call you out on your B.S., inspire you, encourage you, help you think outside the box, and, most importantly, can insert some new energy into your life. A flower needs soil to grow; your growth depends on how much you change ground.

Takeaway Quote: "Your environment can make or break your growth. Surround yourself with people who lift you higher and watch how far you can go."

Gem 33

Energy is Contagious

Energy is like a ripple—it spreads far beyond the source. Whether it's positive or negative, the energy around you has a way of seeping into your life. It's sort of like sitting next to someone with a bad cold. You will "catch their bad vibes" more than you think if they are full of negativity.

But here's the twist—not all energy is terrible. What you allow to influence your world is entirely up to you; positive energy is just as contagious, if not more so. You want to be in an environment with those who speak life to your dreams, push you to improve, and add light to your dark days. They are the people who will help you build, grow, and thrive.

It's not only about protecting your energy, though; it's about being the person who spreads positivity to others. Source of ripples: what ripples are you putting out into the world? What do you raise or drag a person to do? Energy and the world you surround yourself with.

Takeaway Quote: "Energy is contagious–if the people around you aren't building you up, they are tearing you down. Protect your vibe and choose wisely."

Gem 34

Rock Bottom is a Foundation

Hitting rock bottom feels like the end of the road, but it's the start of a new one. When you're at your lowest, you can rebuild from the ground up, more muscular and wiser than before. Rock bottom isn't just a place of defeat—it's a place of clarity.

Here's the twist: when everything falls apart, you see what truly matters. You discover who has your back and what you're made of. What makes it happen is rock bottom, removing the distractions and making you see yourself.

Now, place your bricks one at a time. Make it so big that no storm in life can take it down again. Each brick you remember is an act of resistance, resilience, and resurgence. I'm not lying; it won't be easy to climb back up, but the top view will make it worth it; this is what we want to process.

Takeaway Quote: "Everything happens for a reason. Rock bottom is not the end; it is the ideal foundation to build something stronger. Rise and let it be your story of the comeback."

Gem 35

Stop Blaming, Start Creating

When life doesn't work out in your favor, it's easy to point the finger. It feels like the system, the city and everyone around you are part of one large conspiracy to keep you from winning. But here's the harsh truth: To blame doesn't make any difference. It begins with you, the power to change your life.

But there is this twist: Life may not deal you the winning cards, but that doesn't mean you can't win the game. They say the most incredible opportunity ever is one that you can create for yourself. Even the most minor step you take brings you closer to your goals.

Stop looking for someone to make it right. You have the resources and skills, and you can make moves. The moment you seize the pen of your story is the day you start writing a tale worth telling.

Takeaway Quote: "Stop complaining the world isn't giving you what you don't have. Create opportunities, and your life will never be the same."

Gem 36

Fear Can't Hold You Back

Fear is sneaky. It tells you what to do, doubts your decisions, and keeps you within your comfort zone. But here's the deal with fear: It's not real. It's just a story your brain tells you to protect you; protection doesn't equal success.

Here's the twist: The most significant life regrets don't stem from the risks you took. They come from the risks you didn't take. Fear will be there, but it doesn't have to drive the car." Just recognize that and thank it for trying to keep you safe, then take the wheel.

Taking small steps outside your comfort zone is one of the fastest ways to learn, grow, and shape your desired life. Although fear can try to stop you, it doesn't have to be an insurmountable wall. Take that leap of faith and keep going.

Takeaway Quote: "Fear is a terrible backseat driver. Its blind spots shouldn't dissuade you from getting behind the wheel and following your passions."

Gem 37

The Time is Now

One of the biggest traps is waiting for the right time. The reality is that there's never perfect timing. Life does not wait until you're ready. Opportunities are fleeting; the longer you wait, the gentler they knock.

Here's the twist: messy starts are better than no starts. You don't need all the answers before you begin. The most successful people didn't have it all figured out when they started—they just started.

The time is now. Get in there, make a mess, and trust yourself to pick it up. Opportunities await, so don't allow hesitation to hinder you from having the life you deserve.

Takeaway Quote: "Don't wait for the perfect moment. The time is now, and even messy starts are better than immobility."

Gem 38

Change Your Mindset, Change Your Life

Your mind is your most powerful tool, but it can also be your biggest obstacle. You'll stay stuck if you fill it with doubt, negativity, and excuses. But if you shift your perspective, the world around you will start to move, too.

Here's the twist: your thoughts are like seeds. Whatever you plant will grow. If you plant fear — you will reap timidity. But if you plant belief, you will reap confidence, action, and success. Mindset change is more than positive thinking; it's rooting a belief that moves you to action in your own life.

Start small. Change one negative thought for a constructive one. Celebrate small wins. In the long run, you will retrain your mind to focus on opportunities rather than obstacles.

Takeaway Quote: "You know you can't win with a loser mentality. Change your thinking and watch your world change."

Gem 39

Work Innovatively, Not Just Hard

You must work hard, but that is only part of the equation. Grinding without a plan is like going around in circles. Instead, real progress comes when effort is combined with strategy.

If there's a twist in the plot, working innovatively becomes knowing when to pivot, how to make the most of your time, and where to put your energy. It's about a chessboard king moving while the rest play checkers.

Reassess your positions and ensure that they are consistent with your larger aspirations. You know the grind is supreme, but strategy picks winners from losers.

Takeaway Quote: "Hard work is great, but smart work is better. Put in the effort and the strategy and see how quickly you level up."

Gem 40

Your Past Isn't a Prison

Your history is part of you but only defines you if you allow it to. Every mistake, failure, and heartbreak is a story in your life, not the whole book. You can learn from, grow, and craft a better ending.

Here's the kicker: your past is not a sentence but a teacher. What it teaches you is the secret of your evolution. Use it not to hold you back but to move you ahead. Your past can only ensnare you if you always look back.

Focus on what's ahead. Your best days are yet to be written.

Takeaway Quote: "Your past isn't meant to be a jail cell; it's meant to be a lesson. Learn from, expand beyond, and write a better chapter."

Gem 41

Tune Out the Noise

No matter what you do, people will always have something to say. Whether you're winning, losing, or just living your life, the streets will talk. But here's the thing—their opinions don't pay your bills or build your dreams.

The twist: the noisier the gossip, the bolder your moves. People gossip because they pay attention, and that's a good thing. Use their noise as the background music, not the focus of your success.

But keeping your eyes on your prize is what will silence the noise.

Takeaway Quote: "The streets are going to talk, but what they are saying doesn't matter. Focus on your mission, and let your success be the noise you make."

Gem 42

Discipline Unlocks the Door

Discipline isn't flashy; it's the quiet grind that happens when nobody's watching. It's a commitment to show up, even when you don't like it. Discipline is the secret weapon that turns dreams into reality.

And here's the catch: discipline is the key to the life you've been trying to get into. It isn't only about grinding; it's about being consistent and focused and powering through the tough times. You do this enough, doors open, and life gets turned up a notch in ways you couldn't imagine.

Takeaway Quote: "Discipline is the passcode to unlock everything you've been striving for. Stay consistent and keep showing up. Life will continue to open doors and reveal new possibilities."

Gem 43

Comfort Zones Kill Growth

Comfort feels safe, like a warm blanket on a cold day. But too much comfort can become a trap, keeping you stuck in the same place while life moves forward without you. Growth doesn't happen where you're comfortable—it happens when you challenge yourself, take risks, and step into the unknown.

Staying in your comfort zone feels good now, but it steals from your future. Every time you settle for "good enough," you block yourself from discovering what's possible. Success, adventure, and transformation all exist outside the boundaries of what feels safe.

Here's the thing: discomfort doesn't mean danger. It means change is happening. It means you're pushing past the limits of who you are today to become who you're meant to be. Growth is messy, awkward, and sometimes painful, but it's always worth it.

Start small—try something new, say yes to a challenge, or embrace a little uncertainty. Over time, you'll realize that the fear of stepping out was never as powerful as the reward of moving forward. Comfort is the thief of progress, and life is too short to stay stagnant.

Takeaway Quote: "Comfort zones feel safe, but nothing grows there. Get uncomfortable, take risks, and watch yourself bloom."

Gem 44

Face It to Fix It

You can't fix what you don't face. Life has a way of throwing challenges like financial struggles, strained relationships, or even health issues. It's tempting to avoid these problems, hoping they'll disappear independently, but they won't. Ignoring the tough stuff gives it room to grow.

Here's the twist: facing your problems doesn't make you weak; it makes you powerful. It's not easy to confront what's holding you back, but it's necessary. When you take control of the things you've been avoiding, you shift the power dynamic. You halt being a product of your surroundings and commence being the writer of your narrative.

Start small. Budget if your finances are in turmoil. If a relationship needs repair, have an uncomfortable conversation. If your health is declining, schedule that doctor's appointment. Facing up your problems is powerful. It is the first step to freedom, clarity, and mastery of your life.

Takeaway Quote: "You can't improve what you don't confront. Confront your challenges and reclaim your life."

Gem 45

The Greatest Flex is Peace

In a status-obsessed world emphasizing money, status, and clout, losing touch with what matters most is easy. We pursue things, people, or accomplishments that promise happiness. But the best flex isn't how much money or followers you have; it's waking up without anxiety.

Here's the twist: peace doesn't just happen; it's a choice. It's choosing to let go of grudges, detach from drama, and prioritize your well-being. Peace is knowing who you are and what you want and not letting anything disturb your inner calm. It's walking through chaos with a steady heart, knowing it can't touch you.

Real wealth is being able to smile at the end of the day, regardless of what life has dealt you. It's not about what is in your bank account but what is in your soul. The wealthiest dude in the room is the one whose soundtrack is satisfied, grounded, and unfazed.

Takeaway Quote: "The biggest flex is waking up at ease. And if you think money and clout are cool, true wealth is a calm heart and a fulfilled soul."

Gem 46

Stop Shrinking Yourself

Stop apologizing for being too much. Stop dimming your light to make others comfortable. You were not put on this earth to play small, to hide your gifts, or to shrink into the shadows so someone else can feel more significant.

Here's the twist: Your energy is your superpower. The people who tell you that you are "too much" usually don't know how to deal with your greatness. But that's their problem, not yours. You were meant to shine, take up space, and live boldly. The sun doesn't need to apologize for shining; it just shines.

Lean into who you are. Speak loudly. Laugh freely. Dream unapologetically. The right people will love you for it, and the wrong ones don't count. Then, you can shine and bring hope to others who are struggling.

Takeaway Quote: "Your bright was created to shine, not dull, for another's comfort. Be bold — claim your space, and let the world adjust."

Gem 47

Clap for Yourself

Sometimes, you must be the only one who claps for yourself, and that's okay. Seeking approval from others can make you feel invisible, but self-approval? That's where true power lies. You don't need a crowd to cheer your achievements; you need yourself.

The twist is that this helps build resilience, which means being your cheerleader. When you get good at clapping for yourself, you stop waiting for someone to give you your worth as an audience. You understand that each incremental success is cause for celebration, big or small. Those small victories build to something big."

The ones not clapping now will see later, but by the time they do, you will be so busy winning that you won't care. Applaud at your journey; the world will not do it; applaud: not everybody is born great, even here, as you predicted!

Takeaway Quote: "Sometimes, you will be the only person cheering you on. Celebrate you and keep going."

Gem 48

Re-pot Yourself for Growth

Growth requires the right environment. No matter how strong your potential is, it won't thrive in the wrong soil. If you're surrounded by negativity, jealousy, or stagnation, it's time to re-pot yourself elsewhere.

The twist is that re-potting isn't forsaking where you came from; it's selecting what's in your best interest moving forward. Sometimes, growth means growing away from people, places, and situations that no longer fit who you're becoming. That's not selfish; that is essential.

Seek an inspiring space that fosters personal growth and cause. Be with people who uplift and stretch you. There's no telling how high you grow when you root yourself in the correct soil.

Takeaway Quote: "Your environment matters. If the potting around you does not help you grow, you should re-pot yourself elsewhere."

Gem 49

Patience and Persistence Pay Off

Success is not a race; it's a marathon. It's about regular daily action, even if progress appears sluggish. It takes time, patience, and persistence—where the outliers are born, the dreamers become the doers.

Think of it this way: success is much like a slow-cooked barbecue. It takes time and effort and unrelenting consistency. Every second of waiting and preparation pays off when it's all said and done. But that true magic isn't in speed—it's in the incredible power of deliberate, demanding work done consistently over time. It's about believing in the process and putting in the work when nobody sees it.

Keep low, keep on it, and keep at it. Your moment is coming; when it comes, it'll be sweeter than anything hurried.

Takeaway Quote: "Great things come from patience and perseverance. Keep putting in the work, and know your time is coming."

Gem 50

Your Story is Your Power

Your story is your power. Every one of those chapters - whether triumphant, challenging, or downright messy - has chipped away at you and sculpted the AMAZING human being that you are today. Your triumphs bring you joy, your struggles bring you strength, and your lessons bring you wisdom. All of this creates the masterpiece that is you.

But here's the truth: the chapters you wish to forget — the ones filled with embarrassment, pain, and difficulty — are often the most powerful. Why? These are the raw, vulnerable moments that inspire and motivate others. They show the cracks where the light gets in, where you may have struggled but didn't surrender, and the growth that transformed pain into power. Do not conceal those aspects of your narrative. Lean into them. Own them. They are proof that you can survive, adapt, and thrive. When you own your story, you allow others to own theirs, too. Your story is uniquely yours. No one has lived it, no one can tell it, no one can make it work for them the way you can. That's your power. Use it to share with others, raise up those in need of hope, and change in ways that only you can.

Here's the plot twist: Your life is still unfolding. At each moment, you can take control of your story and make it a more magnificent tale.

Takeaway Quote: "The chapters in your life that you'd like to forget often have the most power. Claim your story—every page—then see how it awakens, heals, and transforms."

Acknowledgments

I'd like to take a moment to acknowledge the incredible entrepreneurs and friends who inspire me daily. Your drive, resilience, and creativity have shown me what's possible and have motivated me to keep pushing forward in my own journey.

To all the dreamers, creators, and doers in my life: thank you for showing me the power of determination and the beauty of pursuing your passion. This book is a testament to the lessons I've learned not just from my own experiences, but from witnessing your greatness.

Here's to all of us reaching new heights and continuing to shine.

Notes & Reflections

Use this space to capture your thoughts, ideas, and personal takeaways from each gem.

_____

_____

_____

_____

_____

_____

_____

_____

_____

_____

_____

_____

_____

_____

www.ingramcontent.com/pod-product-compliance
Lightning Source LLC
Chambersburg PA
CBHW071541120626
46550CB00006B/2530